The Journey called life

Sakshee Sakklani

BookLeaf Publishing

India | USA | UK

Presentation by *BookLeaf Publishing*

Web: www.bookleafpub.com

E-mail: info@bookleafpub.com

ISBN: 9789363305243

First edition 2024

In loving memories of my dear grandparents…

Late Shree Sundar Lal Saklani & Smt Darshani Devi

ACKNOWLEDGEMENT

I would like to acknowledge that this journey has not been possible without the continual support of my family and friends. I owe deep gratitude to my grandparents for giving us the strongest foundation in the form of our parents.

My mom has always been my reality checker. She knows me more than I know myself. She is the force behind that extra mile and I know even when I fall she will be there wrapping me in her arms.

I am thankful to Almighty for giving me the world's best dad. He is my friend, philosopher and guide. He keeps up with all my chitter-chatter while being deeply engrossed in the newspaper. All my wishes, dreams and trips have been taken care of by him. Thank you Dad for being my go-to person always.

I am forever indebted to God for getting me married into a supportive family. My in-laws have been my real motivator. I hardly remember hearing "No" from them ever. They have always been my first audience and testimony of the drafted versions. Heartfelt gratitude for being the pampered girl in both the families. Thank you Maa Papa for not stopping me and letting me unfold my wings.

Lastly, my dearest husband, thank you for accepting me the way I am. Thank you for never stopping me to pursue my hobby and follow my dreams. Thank you for giving me that confidence that no matter what, you would be there.

PREFACE

'The Journey Called Life' is a short collection of poems and narrations. I had not pondered over the title of the book before. When I glanced through the column asking for the book title, this was the first thought and hence the title came to mind. Each one of us is moving, flowing, and hustling with the time. Some joyful moments, others not so joyous, the successes, failures, selections and rejections, the ups and downs, life seems like a sinusoidal graph and we are the points that connect the dots in the graph.

Each one of us has our fair share of this roller coaster ride. Sometimes life seems like a cakewalk and at other times it seems like a huge mountainous rock, difficult to climb. We may crawl, walk, run and pause, but it stops only once and that's forever.

So, let's strive to make this journey as beautiful as possible for ourselves as well as for others. Let's together make this world a beautiful place to live.

THEY

A cause I want to raise my voice for
Not that I am directly involved
But I'm directly attached.

While going to the office every day,
From Karol Bagh to Connaught Place
The smell of burned rubber, the illusion of fog
(smog)
The betel-painted road and the posters pasted
wall.

The queue of autos and chaos of cars
whistles of traffic police, and honk of jaguars
The sweat-bathed rickshaw puller, the
suit-cladded businessman
All pass by but there they stand.

There they play, eat and sleep
All in that one-foot crease
They beg and persuade
Your attention they crave
With the leftovers, they quench their hunger
The clothes you discard become their favourite
attire.

It's humid and hot
Electricity—a luxury they cannot afford
It rains, it lightens
It shakes it thunders
But affix they are, then and there
Like the rock of Gibraltar, they didn't falter.

Unshaken, unmoved
Untouched, undismayed
Firm and strong together they stayed.

No cinemas, no theatres
No shows, no refreshers,
Themselves they laugh
Themselves they dance
The only judge of their performances.

No assumptions, no complains
No cursing, no grudges
Boulevard becomes the playground,
The sky is the only cover,
Bare land is the mattress,
filth and dust are all they wear.

The politics and the policies
The schemes and aids
The MP's and MLA's
All went and came.

The ministers visit
The bureaucratic promises
Files after files
Always under process.

The misery seems to have no end
Hope I can extend a helping hand
The how's and what's
The ifs and buts
Forbid me from taking the first step.

Wish someday, sometime, somehow things
change
They have permanent space with a living wage
Pen in hand and school bag at the back
Ironed uniform and neatly dressed.

There they stand in front of the school gate
The tallest, the merriest
The blameless, the faultless
The pristine, the purest!

God, show me the path
Where my existence remains not merely the
story of my survival
But also the society's upliftment and revival.
May this description become the eye-opener for
all
And perhaps could be my first step of moving
towards the greater call.

Valour

Tough and strong and firm I stand
Oh thunder! Tremble me, if you can.
Tightly to the ground and clenching to the crown
Worn and wounded but unbreakable I am!

Clouds in sky and smogy flare
Misty day and dusty air
Block my eyes but not my vision
Fracture my body, not my reasons.

Down in the plain and up in the hill
Husking outside and Barbie within
Night its moon and dawning is sun
Life is a circle with no u-turn.

Mind your work and live in today
What's ahead and what happened yesterday
Bear no fruits and emanate no results
Fret you up and perturbs your way.

So my dear, let's make a pledge
Not to the world but to ourselves
Stiff and sturdy, undivided we stay
Tremors and quakes, come what may.

Courage and valour are all we have
Angst and agony to be shooed away!

When the pen flows

Embrace imperfections
Rest before rest in peace
Let the naysayers say no
In heart vs mind, I am with heart
Penny vs purpose—the latter
No regrets, live in present
Live and let live, feel free
Liberate your mind and break the chain
I am I, you are YOU, hence no comparison
It's never too late—stop and breathe
No to flaunting
Yes to helping
No to filters
Yes to colours

No to criticism
Yes to optimism
No to gossips
Yes to talks
No to judgements
Yes to justice.

Life

SUCCESS

We don't know what life holds for us.
What might work for one may not work for
another. Everyone has their share of setbacks
and successes. We cannot carve out one specific
plan or a specific formula for one to flourish. It's
circumstantial. Decision-making, timing, mood,
attitude, attributes, and many other factors come
into play. Also, even when everything goes well
or poorly, we may get contradictory results.

Success is subjective. For me, working in a
public sector undertaking is a success; for
others, it could be IAS. For some, carving out an
entrepreneurial journey is a success, while for
others, the child's bright future is a success.

We are the authors of our LIFE book. The DOs I followed could be the DONTs you avoided. In the era of the digitalised world, where content is shared now and then, add filters to your ears and eyes. Every word said is not set in stone.
Accept only what works for you, as YOU know yourself better than anyone.

Employee & Employer

Some tips on improving employee-employer relationships

Create a welcoming, inclusive, and supportive workplace culture where employees feel valued and respected. Celebrate their accomplishments, milestones, and special occasions. Recognise and appreciate your staff for their hard work and achievements. Simple gestures like verbal praise or awards boost their participation.

Weekly discussions over coffee are a must. A small chit-chat other than work is important. It strengthens relationships among employees and fosters a sense of camaraderie. Also, employees get to know that you care beyond your work.

Mistakes to be cautioned in silence, everyone has self-respect. However, displeasure could be shown if intentionally made or casually done. Give employees a degree of control over their work, allowing them to make decisions and making them feel more invested. Micromanagement backfires at times. Offer opportunities for their growth and development. Incentivise wherever possible. Keep them in the forefront when you outperform. They must know that they are important, and it is their victory. When you pour your heart out into something, it gives results sooner or later. If you can deliver, it's your team also who was burning the midnight oil. All days would not be bright and sunny. The cloudy ones are for introspection and realignment. It's never ever a one-way track or one-way communication. Discussion, involvement and participation from office boy and security guard to managers and chief manager. Let your team know you adore them, you care for them, but in the end, you need RESULTS. It's always a mutual relationship.

So TEAM is Together Everyone Achieves More!

Some useful tips:

No one can deny the importance of personal touch in a professional setup.

Celebrations and festivities immediately lighten up the mood.

The team feels more connected and a sense of belongingness to the organisation increases. Inviting family members on special occasions strengthens the employee-employer bond.

Beyond all, festivals are the days of wishes, peace and prosperity in everyone's life. The day is the reminder of FORGET & FORGIVE.

Househelp

I maintain office
She arranges my home
I peep into the files
And she takes care of my doll.

Morning for newspapers
And evening for headlines
Not missing in between
The deadly deadlines.

All seems under control
As you take care of the whole
And I became the superwoman
While you became my backbone.

From dawn to dusk
you toil and work
Giggling-gaggling
Without a smirk.

From office exasperation
To child's botheration
Ginger tea of your hand
Soaks in my all tribulations.

Sometimes I wonder
How it would have been possible
If you have not been there
How would have I climbed up the ladder.

Forever indebted to you
Today, tomorrow and yesterday
For keeping my house in order
You kept your home at bay.

To all the beautiful women
We need one another, time and again
No work is ever big or always small
In the journey called life
We are all trying to hit it head-on.

Let there be gratitude
For what we missed and what we get
Househelp contribution to our life
We shall never forget.

We the Women

The woman in me and the me in her
The care in me and the career in her
The dubious me and the dominion she
Here wrapped in norms and there freedom is
free.

Submissive voice and eyes down
Household chores I perform
Fiery eyes and I raise my voice
Countdown to patriarchy, I stand for reform.

Simple me and sassy you.
Draped in saree and formals for you
Busy bee and no time for me
House in order and unarranged me.

Neatly dressed and evenly tucked
After work an hour I deduct
Not for anyone but for myself I keep
Sixty minutes of meditation and calm breathe.

Round the clock all night and day
Work in office and homework awaiting the way
Equal we work but unequal are our pays
Child I rear and promotions you embrace.
Unacknowledged work and rare recognition
Apologies for forgetting but again repetition.

Dear beautiful ladies, do not forget we are all
one
The misses in me from you I learn
Different may be the playgrounds
But similar are the plays,
Both you and me always commonly face.

Not to worry my dearest darlings
The more we're suppressed the higher we rise
Sisters, friends, colleagues and mother
Whatsoever the relation, we are all one and
together.

Let unity be our strength
Love and mutual respect our guiding force
Who is going to stop us?
When each other's support we owe!

Words of Wisdom

Sometimes we keep hustling just to reach somewhere but we often forget that it's always the journey that's more beautiful than the destination itself.

Want to contribute something to society or a greater cause? Do not need to go far. There are many people around us, among us who need a healing hand and a listening ear. Many such exist in our families, extended families and neighbours.

Taking time from your hectic schedule and attending your friend's book launch or tired from the office but teaching your neighbour's child or forwarding the messages of your aunt's NGO to the rest of your network.

Many such are the small contributions we all can make to other's lives and one's life as well. An act of pure kindness uplifts our conscience and soothes our minds too.

Why taking a break can help?

It breaks the monotonicity. Sometimes we repetitively follow the same pattern and desire different outcomes. A BREAK breaks this pattern. You get an opportunity to see, observe and perceive things differently. For some time you are out of the productivity bubble and enjoy the little joys of life. If you prefer travelling in your break time, then you explore the Wonders of the World. You witness different cultures, meet different people and exchange different thoughts. The body and mind get recharged for the coming days in the office and at home.

Lastly, in the break time, You are YOU. The naughty YOU, the silly YOU, the carefree YOU and the kid in YOU.

Confused on weekends?

Me: As the weekend already started you have two choices—

A) Work on the #dreams #plan #ideas you have. Work on the #community #project you want to build or start.

B) Worked hard the entire week so time to #relax and #retreat. You can travel, and meet friends and relatives. You can also go for a movie.

What to choose option one or option two?

I think it's easy to convince your heart to go with the latter. But those who have made their dreams a reality might have opted for the first. Success does not come easily. It's not a cakewalk to convert your vision into reality. Discipline and focus are foremost.

As it's aptly said, "The choices you make TODAY shape your TOMORROW."

Women Reservation Act

Census 2011: The literacy rate in the country is 74.04 per cent, 82 for males and 65 for females.

Currently, less than 15 per cent of women MP (highest percentage ever) in Lok Sabha, 14 per cent in Rajya Sabha and less than 10 per cent in many States (9 per cent in Uttarakhand).

As per the Inter-Parliamentary Union Report 2019, out of a total of 193 countries of the world, India ranks 149 in terms of women in Parliament (this is when India is one of the top five economies of the world).

Yes, we needed a Women's Reservation Act.

Reservation does not mean that women are less capable, reservation is our rightful compensation for the historic social, political and economic deprivation.

To all the women out there:

Free up your mind. Free from This, That, Why, What and When.

For a moment keep things aside and think just about yourself.

Take out time for your leisure walk, coffee chats or singing and dancing.

Sometimes it's ok to close your eyes and relax. Sky is not going to fall if you are idle for a while and not doing anything.

This time when you are going for shopping, buy something for yourself too and buy what you want to wear, not what others want you to be dressed in.

Next time when someone says you have gained weight or lost weight or looking older or darker just smile and pass it off. You do not need others' validation to know that You are beautiful inside and out.

👉 Do not give a damn about other's opinions or judgement. Let your conscience be your guide.

👉 Dear Women, Love yourself for who you are or for who you are not. You do not need to be perfect all the time. Embrace your imperfections, sharpen your strength and work on your weakness.

More power to

✴ The ferocious you

✴ The fearless you

✴ The fabulous you!

The more you shut our voice, the louder it comes.

Don't consider our silence as our weakness.

Beware!

Real Life Story.. An Honest Confession

Never hesitate on your journey. As long as you are taking baby steps, you are in action mode. Only thinking and no execution takes you nowhere. Do not be hesitant to try and learn something new. What more can happen than not succeeding? As it's said, "It's better to try and fail than to never try at all."

Last year, me and my husband were just having a conversation with one of our in-house guests at the hotel. We usually end up creating a bond with our long-term guests. This time, the only difference was that we recorded the conversation. With his permission, I uploaded it to YouTube.

There was no proper mic, light, or camera. We recorded it on one phone and captured it on another. As it was an open area, the recorded voice was not clear. I find video editing cumbersome, so I uploaded the raw video.

Guess what! Just a few days ago, I found that the video reached one thousand views.

This makes me think that though there have been enormous changes due to technology, some things never change. Amidst all the digital marketing hacks, hashtags, and Instagram filters, there is always an audience for unfiltered emotions. Simplicity and originality never fade out.

The organic, the natural, and the raw have their innate beauty.
Time passes, software updates, technology changes and emotions remain.

Topic: Job Satisfaction

Sometimes we just don't see things close to us.
To put it in another way, sometimes we just don't acknowledge the things we easily get.

So time for an #honest confession—

2013 - passed out college with flying colours.

2014 - faced the first competition of my life #IBPS PO, and cracked it on the first attempt without coaching. This means I achieved financial independence at the age of 21. So, as per #society norms, I was quite settled with a secured government job.

2015 - Within one year, I was done. The excitement of an independent life was gradually vanishing.

2016-2018- Cribbing became a regular affair. Desperately wanted to explore another world of opportunities. Frustration was creeping in, now at a comparatively faster rate.

2018 - 2020 - Got married and promoted simultaneously. Banking being a transferable job, me and my husband were in a long-distance relationship. After the office, I used to devote some time to books and preparation. So, I was constantly juggling between work, office, home and an aspirant life.

2020 - 2022 - Anxiety and #stress levels are
now on the higher side. I was devoid of emotion.
In retrospect, I could say I was emotionally
numb. Round the clock my mind was on work,
academics and better #career options.

2022 - Present - My spouse's transfer request
was accepted. I am heading a semi-urban
branch. My husband runs a holiday home. After
the office, I assisted him in #recycling waste
plastic bottles, cans, containers, etc into
beautiful planters and wall decor. Gradually, the
thirst for a better world and better opportunities
started sinking in. I am now in a much
#balanced zone. I am not madly chasing
something. I am not turning my eyes away from
seeing the better side of my job. I am not doing
all this intentionally. It's just happening.

All I am doing is just slowing down. Now, I am
flowing with time. Life seems much calmer this
way.

She

She means peace but wins the war
She is soft but knows when to roar
She is care but not careless
She is carefree but not casual
She is glamour and also an officer in uniform
Boss in the office and house chores she performs
She is all her mind she is all her heart
She knows to stop and when to kickstart.

Golden Rule Of Moderation

No one is fully good or entirely bad
All white and deep black
Makes life dull and dead.

No praise and only critic
Makes one no less than a narcissist
Too much noise and drop-down silence
Perturbs one peace and
disturbs the balance.

Different people and different the characters
After a hot scorching summer
Comes the cold deserted winter.

Follow the teachings of Buddha
And the golden rule of moderation
Let's not fall prey to passion
And be a victim of temptation .

Let there be no judgement
The judiciary has its role
Let's embrace one another
Let's become one and whole.

Do not slog and do not haste
Things happen at their own pace.
Focus on karma and beloved actions
Conserve energy of instant reaction
Half of the misery seems to vanish
If one delays the response timing.

Let's balance be our target
And dhyana our goal
Life will be blissful
When everyone is committed to one's role.

Quotes

It's not the pen that writes
It is the soul that speaks.

There is ONE supreme power/energy.
Most are with the strong ones, you empower the
other.

When the leader dies
The World cries
(written after the demise of the Late Shri Bipin
Rawat, Former Chief of Army Staff of the
Indian Army).

The mind wants progress
The heart wants pauses
The tussle between the two
Is balanced by the few
Those who know the key
Are happy, merry and glee.

Do not doubt your dream
Nurture it with your efforts and hard work
And one day you will realize
It is not a dream anymore
It has become your reality.

Let YOU define yourself
Nobody else.

प्यार

सोच रही थी क्या मैं लिखूं
यूँ अदब से ज़िक्र किसका मैं करूं
करीब से जिसे देखा है मैंने
कि ज़िंदगी के फ़लसफ़े के बारे में लिखूं।

इसी कशमकश में ही थी
कि नज़रों के सामने धुंधला सा एक चित्र आया
खूब चर्चाएं, सब पर हुईं
पर दास्तां-ए-मोहब्बत का ज़िक्र कभी ना आया।

ख्याल आया आज, ख्वाबों की इन लहरों के साथ ही
रुख कर लिया जाए
पन्नों पर स्याही अबकी बार इश्क की फरमाई जाए
समाज की शर्म और अपनों का भरम
सब छोड़ कर, दिल के गलियारों में आज दस्तक दी
जाए।

खूबसूरत सा कुछ ये एहसास है,
ज़िंदगी उसके साथ लगती एक हसीन ख्वाब है
ना आस-पास उसके होने पर
लगता खामोश मानो ये सारा संसार है।

जब पाऊँ उसे अपने से दूर
कमबख्त ये समय भी तो रुक जाता है
चिड़ियाएं जल्दी चहचहाती हैं सवेरे को
और ये सूरज भी तो देर शाम ही ढल पाता है।

हर बात उसकी यूँ अच्छी लगे
आंखें उसकी सच्ची लगे
सुबह शाम उसके ख्वाबों में
बस डूब जाने का यूँ मन करता है।

हर एक उसके कहे लफ़्ज़ पर
देर तक खोई हुई रहती हूं
ज़रा सी उसकी आहट पर
घंटो उठ मैं बैठती हूं
खाना गर ना उसका समय पर
तो निवाला मैं भी नहीं निगल पाती हूं
नींद गर ना पूरी उसकी
तो बैचैन रात अपने नाम लिख जाती हूं।

अपने को यूँ भूलकर
कबसे उसकी यूँ होने लगी हूं
पता ही नहीं चला कब मैं से हम
और हम से तुम मैं बन गई हूं।

खुशियां ही खुशियां उसके दामन में
और उसके सौ दर्द मेरे नाम
फूले फले वो सदैव हमेशा
और मेरी झोली में सारे उसके दुख तमाम।

खुदा से ये ही इल्तजा है
खूब इनायत बक्शे तुम्हें
मैं रहूँ या ना रहूं पास तुम्हारे
मन का ये मिलन तो सदियों का है।

राधा रुक्मणी कुछ भी समझो
कृष्ण तुम मेरे पूरे हो
मीरा की भक्ति में
चाहे मिलन मुक्कमल या अधूरा हो
साथ लंबा या छोटा सही
अब किसे ये डर ये फिकर।

तुम्हारी जीवन संगिनी मैं
और तुम मेरे हमराही, हमसफर।

आम आदमी

बिजली विभाग के दफ़्तर तक
पानी के बिल भरने तक
हाउस टैक्स जमा करने तक
दौड़ता रहता है आम आदमी।

कभी हेलमेट न पहनने पर
कभी सीट की पेटी ना बांधने पर
कभी बाएं से ओवरटेक करने पर
तो कभी इंश्योरेंस एक्सपायर होने पर
चालान भरता रहा आम आदमी।

कभी यह काउंटर
तो कभी वह चैंबर
कभी जज की छुट्टी
तो कभी बड़े साहब का इंतज़ार
करता रहता है आम आदमी।

शर्ट-पैंट पहनें
पसीना बहाए
हाथ में फाईलें लेकर
डिपार्टमेंट की दौड़ लगाए।

किसी को न तरस उसपर आए
खून-पसीने की कमाई नंबर लगवाने पर लुटाए
कभी समय से पर्ची बनवाने को
कभी तारीख जल्दी दिलवाने को
कभी मामला निपटाने को
सब उसकी जेब हल्की करायें
तरस ना आम आदमी पे किसी को आये।

बचा-कुचा जो अब घर लाए
सरकार उसपर नज़रें गड़ाए
टैक्स न जमा करने के नाम पर
फिर उस पर जुर्माना लगाए।

ए समाज तेरी कैसी ये लीला
सारा कानून आम आदमी के लिए तू बनाए
जो सेठ, साहूकार हैं, पैसे जिनपे अपार हैं
उनके हिस्से न कोई जुर्माना-चालान आए।

कहने के लिए तो
अनुसंधान सरकार ने खूब हैं बनाए
परंतु उनके पालन की सारी ज़िम्मेदारी
सिर्फ आम आदमी के हिस्से आए।

घर में बड़ों की
दफ़्तर में बॉस की
समाज में पुलिस की
तो कभी कोई विभाग की
हर जगह वो सुनता जाए
किसी को आम आदमी पर तरस न आए।

बस करो - महिलाओं पर व्यंग

आज सवाल मेरा समाज के उस वर्ग से है, जिसे हम महिला के नाम से जानते हैं। और खास तौर से उन महिलाओं से है जो अपने आप को कम आंकती हैं। बस करो और बंद करो। लाचारी के तराजू में अपने आप को तोलना, वह घूंघट के पर्दे से बाहर की हसीं नज़ारा देखना, पति को समय पर खाना परोसने में अपनी जीत समझना। बच्चो के सपनों में अपना संसार ढूंढना, समाज को खुश करने के लिए अपनी खुशियों का गला घोटना।

जींस पहनना चाहती हो, तो पहनो!
क्यों साड़ी में अपने आप को लपेटे रहती हो, ऑफिस साड़ी पहनकर जाना चाहती हो तो क्यों ट्राउसर पहने जाती हो।बाल खुले करना चाहती हो तो फिर क्यों पोनीटेल कर लेती हो। संगीत तुम्हे पसंद हुआ करता था तो क्यों आज बर्तनों की खनखन और चूड़ियों की छनचन में संतुष्ट हो जाते हो। चालींस साल पुरानी

अपनी शादी की तस्वीरों को देखकर अपनी जवानी के
दिन याद करती हो, तो क्यों आज सजने-संवरने से
फिर संकोच करती हो। अपने दोस्तों संग गुज़रे दिन
आज भी तुम्हें मुंह ज़बानी याद है तो क्यों उनसे
मिलने में आज तुम आनाकानी करती हो।

अलमारी के किसी कोने में अपनी पुरानी डायरी
दफनाए बैठी हो।
जिन पन्नों को किसी समय तुमने अपने मन की
स्याही से पिरोया होगा उन शब्दों की महक कैसे तुम
भूल बैठी हो।
बच्चों की किताबों में जब तुम चित्र बनाती हो।
कितनी खुबसूरती से तुम पंखों में रंग भरती हो, खुले
आसमां को नीला करती हो। फिर क्यों तुम खुद वो
उड़ान भरने को डरती हो।

बंद करो और बस करो
खुलकर सांस लेने का प्रयास करो अपनी मांगे मांगने
की ज़िद करो
पीछे चलते रहने का नहीं आगे बढ़ चढ़कर अपना
योगदान करो
तुम्हारी दबी आवाज़ गुमनामी में कहीं खो जाएगी,
चीखकर जब तक तुम हाहाकार ना करो।

परिवार की ही नहीं अपनी खुशियों की भी ज़िम्मेदारी
लो
घर की गृहलक्ष्मी ही नहीं समाज की अर्थव्यवस्था में
भी भागीदारी लो।
एक दूसरे की खामी नहीं एक दूजे को प्रोत्साहित करो।

एक महिला की जीत पूरे महिला वर्ग की जीत है,
ढोल नगाड़ों के संग हौसला अफ़ज़ाई करो।

सब एक साथ एक जुट होकर
साथ साथ दो कदम बढ़ाएं,
अगर एक लड़खड़ाए तो दूजा हाथ थमाए।
हम स्त्रियां एक दूसरे की ताकत हैं,
साथ चलो तो पृथ्वी का कोई प्राणी हमें ललकार ना
पाए।
आपस में ही अगर घिट-पिट करें
तो तीसरा विश्व युद्ध छिड़ जाए।
तीसरा विश्व युद्ध छिड़ जाए।

स्याही

बेज़ुबानों की वाणी
मैं बूढ़ों का सहारा,
मत समझो मुझे कमज़ोर कड़ी
कितनों पर मैं स्याही ने अपना कहर डाला।

सच की साथी
गरीबों की लाठी,
तोलों में ना तुलने वाली
मैं तो बस मामूली स्याही हूं।

दग़ाबाज़ों की धांधली
अमीरों का अहंकार,
मेरे कलम के प्रकोप से
ना बच पाया कोई सेठ साहूकार।

गांधी जी की लाठी मैं
विद्वानों का स्वाभिमान,
मत उलझना मुझसे तू
ऐ छल कपटी इंसान।

युद्ध का अंत मैं
नीतियों का स्तंभ मैं,
ज्ञानी का कवच मैं
अज्ञानी का वध मैं।

ईमानदारी की राह में जो चले
उसका सारथी मैं बन जाऊं,
सुबह दिन रात जो एक करे
उसे कलेक्टर मैं बनवाऊँ।

शक्ति मेरी जो तू ना समझे
हर पल फिर पछताएगा,
कलम के मेरे एक फैसले से
जीवन भर कारावास में फिर बिताएगा।

सच की साथी
गरीबों की लाठी ,
पैसों में ना बिकने वाली
मैं तो बस मामूली स्याही हूं।

बचपन

परियों संग मैं खेल रही थी
आंख मिचौली छुपन-छुपाई,
गुलाबी फ्रॉक, सिर पर मुकुट
आज बनी राजकुमारी मैं इठलाई।

इतने में ही नींद खुली की
नाश्ता बाबूजी का लगाओ,
छोटे भाई का बस्ता लगाकर
तुम भी अपने स्कूल जाओ।

चल पड़ी मैं साइकिल पर
सहेलियों संग फिर दौड़ लगाऊं,
उछलते-कूदते करते-करते
कक्षा में फिर आखिरी जाऊं।

मास्टर जी पूछे पहाड़े तो
झटपट उनको मैं बतलाऊं,
छुट्टी होने पर फिर
गेट के बाहर मैं इमली खाऊं।

बाबूजी जब दफ़्तर से आएं
साथ अपने सैर कराएं,
मां के हाथ की चाय पीकर
होमवर्क फिर वह हमें करवाएं।

चंदा मामा आते ही
मां हमें खाना खिलाए,
गरमा-गरम दूध पीकर
लोरियों संग फिर मां सुलाए।

तीस बरस बीत गए
बीत गई वो चांदनी रातें,
सबको खाना परोसने बाद
आखिरी आज फिर नंबर आए।

फटी हुई एड़ी और बिखरे हुए बाल
ज़िम्मेदारियों का बोझ, घर के कामकाज,
अधेड़ उम्र बीत गई
बीत गई वह बेपरवाह यादें
आज भी चेहरे पर मुस्कान लाती
बचपन की वो सुनहरी यादें।

आज़ाद पंछी

खुले आसमां में उड़ना चाहूं
कटी पतंग जैसा फिरना चाहूं,
झिलमिल तारों से मिल मिलकर
फिर चांद जैसे मैं चमकना चाहूं।

चिड़िया जैसे पंख फैलाकर
बेफ़िक्री में चक्कर लगाऊं,
सावन की रिमझिम बारिश में
मोर तरह मैं थिरकना चाहूं।

बतख जैसे छपक-छपक कर
तालाब मैं पार कर आऊं,
तोते जैसा मिठू-मिठू बोलकर
कोयल जैसा गीत मैं गाऊँ।

बेड़ियां मुझे भाये नहीं
सोने का पिंजरा परेशान करे,
सारे ताले आज तोड़कर
खुले आसमां में उड़ना चाहूं।

नई शुरुआत

प्यार तू अपने आप से कर
अपने उन सपनों से कर
जो खुली आंखों से भी देख कर
पूरा होगा, है विश्वास मगर।

हिम्मत तू कभी ना हार
हौसलों को अपने बुलंद कर
रुक, गिर, पर थम नहीं मगर
फिर से नई शुरुआत कर।

तोड़ दे ये बेड़ियाँ
जो तूने खुद से खुदी को पहनाई है
दुनिया कब किसी की हुई है
जो रट तूने ये लगाई है।

ज़माना क्या कहेगा
गर, ये ही तू सोचता रहेगा
तो घुट-घुट के कैसा ये जीना
जो तूने अपने के लिए खुद ही चुना।

इसका ज़िम्मेदार
सिर्फ तूमेरे यार
क्योंकि अपनी ज़िंदगी के फ़ैसले के लिए
तूने रुख लिया दुनिया वालों का बार-बार।

सुन, अभी भी कुछ बिगड़ा नहीं
जब जागो तब भी सवेरा है
कब, कैसे, किसे, कौन
कहाँ, तू इसमें उलझा है।

छोटी सी तो ज़िंदगानी
और दो-चार पलों का कारवां
अगर, मगर, कैसे, भला
बुझा मत तू ये पहेलियां।

मन की तू आवाज़ सुन
क्या तुझसे ये कहता है
बचपन में जो लगता अच्छा तुझे
क्या आज भी ख़ुशी वैसी दे जाता है।

हाँ, अगर इसका जवाब है
तो क्यों नहीं वो कर पाता है
चंद रुपयों के लिए क्यूँ
तू अपना सुकून बेच आता है।

ये पैसे की दुनिया में
सब एक माया जाल है
जीने के लिए मेरे यार
काफ़ी रोटी, कपड़ा या मकान है।

अँधेरा है अगर कहीं, कल सवेरा भी होगा
परेशानियाँ अगर आज, कल समाधान भी होगा
तू अकेला नहीं यहाँ इस भीड़ में, मेरे यार
तुझ सा हाल और न जाने कितनों का होगा।

मत पड़ ये प्यार, इश्क या मोहब्बत में
सपने अपना साकार कर
जब प्यार करेगा अपने आप से तू पहले
तब भी तो लुटा पाएगा किसी और पर।

ज़िंदगी बार-बार यूँ मौका नहीं देती
आज, अभी और ये सही वक्त
दिल खोलकर अपनी बात रख
आवाज़ अपनी कर सख्त
एक बार जो अब ठान लिया
मुड़कर फिर देखना नहीं
तेरा मुक्कदर तू ही है
फिर से आश्रय ढूँढ़ना नहीं।

फरिश्ता आसमान से नहीं कोई आएगा
धक्का कोई कब तक ही मार पाएगा
अपनी कहानी के रचयिता हम ही हैं
मांझी, तेरी कश्ती को पार, अब तू ही लगाएगा।

बिना खून-पसीने नहीं होते सपने साकार
कोशिश कर लो चाहे हज़ार
दिन-रात को एक करना होगा
लहू जिस्म से बहाना होगा।

शंख की आगाज़ पर
अब तू नई शुरुआत कर
सपने अपने साकार कर
और लंबी सी ये उड़ान भर।

आज नहीं तो कल फल मिलेगा
गुलिस्तां तेरा ज़रूर खिलेगा
मौहल्ले के बच्चों का हीरो तू होगा
चाय पे चर्चा का किस्सा तू होगा
रूबरू तुझसे फिर अखबारों पे होगा
इन महफिलो में तेरा इंतज़ार सा होगा
तेरी एक झलक के दीदार के लिए
लंबा सा फिर कोई कहीं काफिला होगा।

मेरी मां

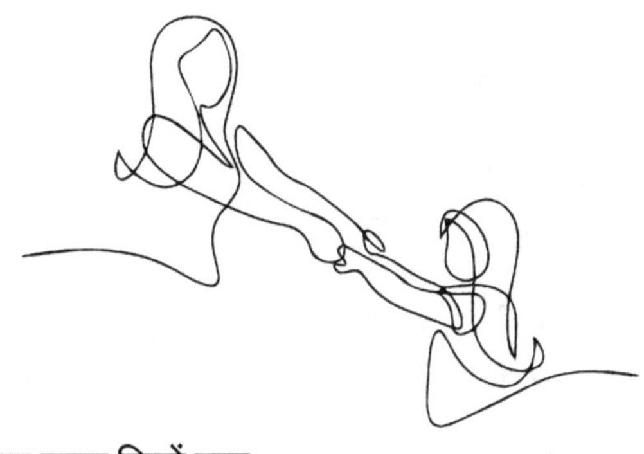

आज बहुत दिनों बाद
कुछ बयां करने का मन हुआ
यूं तो समय कम ना था
पर ज़िंदगी की भाग दौड़ में
कुछ उलझते ही चले गए!
ख्याल आया कि चलो आज
ये उलझे तानो बानों को
स्याही के ज़रिए सुलझाया जाए।

यूं तो मां की याद
यत्र तत्र सर्वत्र आती है,
पर आज उनके आस-पास
ना होने का एहसास
कुछ ज़्यादा सा ही है।

लोग कहते हैं अपनी मां की तरह दिखती हो
कैसे समझाऊं दिखती ही नहीं,
उन्हीं की तरह तो हूं।

यूं रफ्तार से काम करना
भावनाओं के बवंडर में घंटो उलझे रहना
कुछ कर गुज़रने की कोशिश
कुछ नया सीखने की चाह
यूं आसमान छू जाने की तमन्ना
और अपनों के लिए
मर-मिट जाने का उत्साह

सब स्वयं से ही तो आया है,
सब उन्हीं से ही तो आया है।

हां, पूरी सही नहीं है
गुस्से से गुज़रती वह
बाज़ार से लाना कुछ और
लेकर कुछ और है लाती वह।

खाना बनाती है
पर कुछ खास शौक नहीं
हां, साज-सज्जा को लेकर
एकदम पारखी नज़र वह।

अपनी गलती न माने जो
ऐसा उसका मिज़ाज,
पापा से है मनवाती बातें
पूरे घर पर उन्हीं का राज।

समझे अपने आप को खूब स्यानी वह
पर छल कपट न समझ पाए
साफ दिल और ज़िंदादिली
पर जुबां से हरी मिर्च वह।

गौरवान्वित महसूस करती
कि बच्चों को पढ़ा लिखा लिया है,
शादी भी उनकी मनपसंद
और दामाद तो उनके हीरा हैं।

अपने में ही इठलाती
अपने में ही बतलाती,
परेशानियों को अपनी
हंसी के पीछे है छुपाती,
डांटती फटकारती खूब ही हमको
पर पास ना होने पर
याद बहुत आती।

जब भी पढ़ाई में जी ना लगता
कहती थी कोई बात नही
छत में टहलती मेरे साथ,
और मेरे अच्छे अंकों की
कोई ख्वाहिश नहीं।

कहती ज़्यादा मत पढ़ा करो
थोड़ा घूम भी लिया करो,
मस्तिष्क भी आराम चाहता है
ज़्यादा ज़ोर मत दिया करो।

इस चकाचौंध की दुनिया में
उनकी याद कुछ ज़्यादा सी आती,
उनकी बेफ़िक्री बातें
आज भी सुकून हैं लाती।

ऐसी अजीबो गरीब वह
और निराली उनकी कहानी
उनमें से एक यह
खुद उनकी बेटी की ज़ुबानी।